D0506873

GUMDROP BOOKS - Bethany, Missouri

The Phoenicians

The Phoenicians

Pamela Odijk

Silver Burdett Press

Acknowledgments

The author and publishers are grateful to the following for permission to reproduce copyright photographs and prints:

ANT/NHPA pp. 12, 13, 17; Bettman Archive p. 38; Michael Holford p. 26; The Mansell Collection pp. 19, 20; Ron Sheridan's Photo-Library pp. 14, 15, 16, 18, 21, 23, 24, 28, 29, 30, 34, 37, 40 and the cover photograph.

While every care has been taken to trace and acknowledge copyright, the publishers tender their apologies for any accidental infringement where copyright has proved untraceable. They would be pleased to come to a suitable arrangement with the rightful owner in each case.

First published 1989 by
THE MACMILLAN COMPANY OF AUSTRALIA PTY LTD
107 Moray Street, South Melbourne 3205
6 Clarke Street, Crows Nest 2065

Adapted and first published in the United States in 1989
by Silver Burdett Press, Englewood Cliffs, N.J.

Library of Congress Cataloging-in-Publication Data

Odijk, Pamela, 1942–
      The Phoenicians / Pamela Odijk.
         p.   cm.—(The Ancient world)
      Includes index.
      Summary: Discusses the civilization of the Phoenicians,
including the hunting, medicine, clothing, religion, laws, legends,
and recreation.
      1. Phoenicians—Juvenile literature.
[1. Phoenicians.] I. Title.   II. Series:
Odijk, Pamela, 1942–   Ancient world.
DS81.035   1989
939′.44—dc20   89-33860
      ISBN 0-382-09891-9   CIP
                                                               AC

The Phoenicians

Contents

The Phoenicians: Timeline

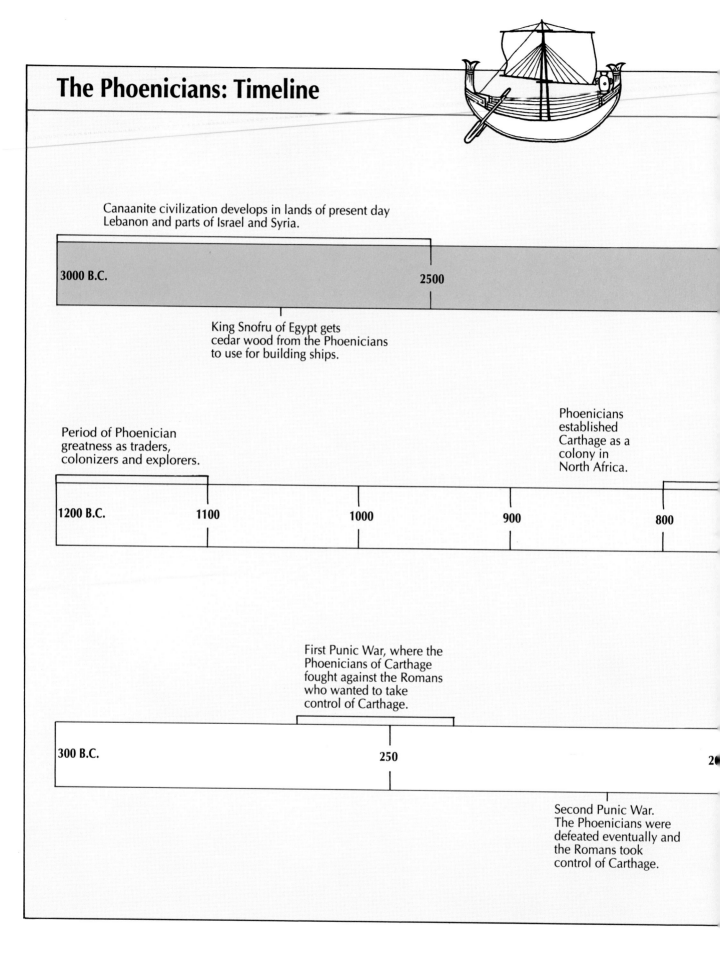

Canaanite civilization develops in lands of present day Lebanon and parts of Israel and Syria.

3000 B.C.   **2500**

King Snofru of Egypt gets cedar wood from the Phoenicians to use for building ships.

Period of Phoenician greatness as traders, colonizers and explorers.

Phoenicians established Carthage as a colony in North Africa.

1200 B.C.   **1100**   **1000**   **900**   **800**

First Punic War, where the Phoenicians of Carthage fought against the Romans who wanted to take control of Carthage.

300 B.C.   **250**   **2**

Second Punic War. The Phoenicians were defeated eventually and the Romans took control of Carthage.

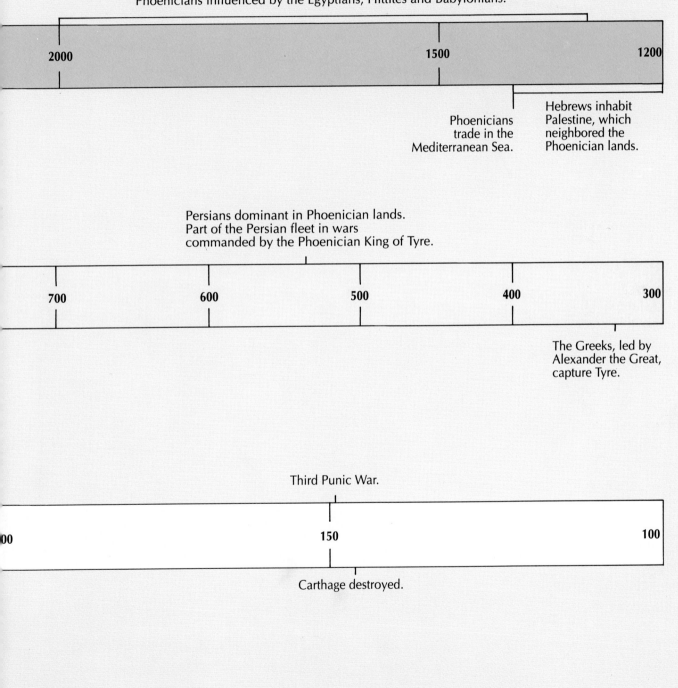

Phoenicians influenced by the Egyptians, Hittites and Babylonians.

| 2000 | 1500 | 1200 |

Phoenicians trade in the Mediterranean Sea.

Hebrews inhabit Palestine, which neighbored the Phoenician lands.

Persians dominant in Phoenician lands.
Part of the Persian fleet in wars
commanded by the Phoenician King of Tyre.

| 700 | 600 | 500 | 400 | 300 |

The Greeks, led by Alexander the Great, capture Tyre.

Third Punic War.

| 00 | 150 | 100 |

Carthage destroyed.

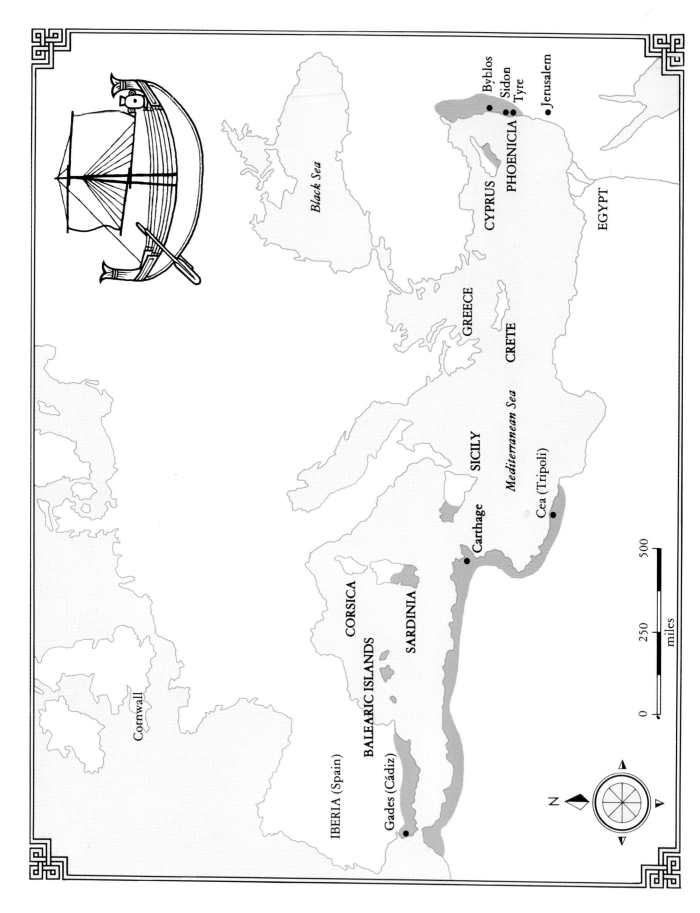

Black Sea

Mediterranean Sea

Byblos
Sidon
Tyre
•Jerusalem

CYPRUS

PHOENICIA

EGYPT

GREECE

CRETE

SICILY

Cea (Tripoli)

Carthage

CORSICA

SARDINIA

BALEARIC ISLANDS

IBERIA (Spain)

Gades (Cádiz)

Cornwall

N

0   250   500

miles

The Phoenicians: Introduction

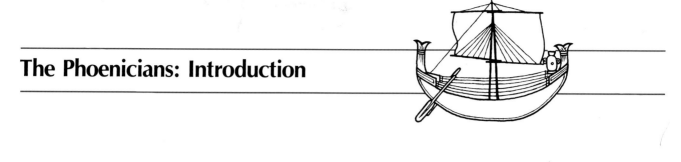

The Phoenicians occupied the land that is called Lebanon today, and parts of Syria and Israel. The ancient name for this area was Canaan (Kena'an) and they called themselves **Canaanites** or Kena'ani. In Hebrew the word *kena'ani* also means "merchant." This describes the Phoenicians well.

The Canaanite civilization began to develop in what is now modern-day Lebanon in about 3000 B.C. The Egyptians, Babylonians, and Hittites controlled Phoenicia until about 1200 B.C. Over the next 400 years or so, Phoenician fortunes flowered as they became the major traders and colonizers in the Mediterranean world. Their ships carried raw materials such as their highly prized cedar trees, copper, and minerals, as well as manufactured goods such as fine purple cloth, wooden furniture, carved ivory, metal work, and glass. Their people established trading colonies around the Mediterranean Sea from Phoenicia to Spain, and those in the west expanded to become the Carthaginian Empire. Their ships ventured beyond the Mediterranean on voyages around the continent of Africa and probably northward to Cornwall in England.

The Phoenicians worshiped many local gods. El was the father of their gods and Ashirat of the Sea (biblical Asherah) was his wife. Other gods included Baal, the storm and war

Phoenician sea traders landing a cargo.

god who was also called Melcart in the city of Tyre, and both Astarte and Anath, goddesses of fertility. Ancient gods often played many roles, and in time became identified with similar gods of other nations such as Egypt and Greece.

The Phoenician alphabet of twenty-two letters was in use in the fifteenth century B.C. The Greeks later adopted this alphabet and created a model alphabet for many others to use.

Gradually the Phoenician city-states were attacked and conquered. Phoenicia fell to the Assyrians in 860 B.C., the Babylonians in 612 B.C., the Persians in 538 B.C., the Greeks in 332 B.C., and the Romans in 64 B.C. The culture of the conquerors gradually began to overshadow the Phoenician culture in the east, although it survived in the west well into Roman times.

However, the eastern Phoenician cities did not completely die all at once. Tyre and Sidon existed as independent cities from 120 and 111 B.C., respectively, and even when the Romans gained control of the Phoenician cities in 64 B.C., Tyre, Sidon, and Tripoli were still characteristically Phoenician. Eventually Alexandria in Egypt became the leading trade center instead of Tyre.

Some Important Dates and Events

Approximate Dates	What Happened	Approximate Dates	What Happened
3000–2500 B.C.	Phoenician people build towns in present-day Lebanon and parts of Syria and Israel.	332 B.C.	Alexander the Great captured Tyre.
2000–1100 B.C.	Egyptian, Babylonian, and Hittite influence on the Phoenicians.	264–241 B.C.	First Punic War. The Phoenicians in Carthage fought the Romans for control of western Mediterranean.
1300–1200 B.C.	The Hebrews enter Palestine (Canaan), which neighbored the Phoenician lands.	218–201 B.C.	Second Punic War. Hannibal crossed the Alps. Carthage eventually defeated.
1200–700 B.C.	Period of Phoenician greatness as traders, colonizers, and explorers.	149 B.C.	Third Punic War. The Romans took control of Carthage.
860–538 B.C.	Phoenicians conquered by the Assyrians, Babylonians, and Persians.	146 B.C.	Carthage destroyed.
850 B.C.	Phoenicia founded Carthage in North Africa.	64 B.C.	The Romans took control of remaining Phoenician cities.

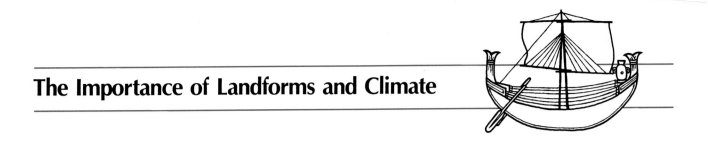

The Importance of Landforms and Climate

The land once occupied by the Phoenicians was bounded by the Mediterranean Sea on the west and the mountains of Lebanon stretching for 100 miles (160 kilometers) in the east. These peaks rise to 10,130 feet (3,088 meters) in some places. The distance from the mountains to the sea is as little as 7 miles (12 kilometers) in some places and as wide as 30 miles (49 kilometers) in others. In between are rocky **promontories,** which stretch to the sea with small valleys in between. In these valleys small springs and rivers run in winter but dry up during the summer. The land available for settlement is fertile and can be farmed.

The people who settled in the fertile valleys were isolated from each other and felt they belonged to their own community rather than to a united country. Because the mountains formed a high barrier in the east, they protected the Phoenicians from invaders. They also prevented the Phoenicians from expanding their lands beyond the mountain range or from having contact with neighboring cultures. The Phoenicians naturally turned to the sea as the easiest way to explore, and later, to expand their territory and to trade.

Phoenicia's climate is warm to hot with dry summers and wet winters. About 40 inches (1,000 millimeters) of rain falls each year. The high mountains are snow capped in winter and spring.

During Phoenician times deposits of marble, **lignite,** and iron could be found in the mountains, and fine sand provided a material for use in the Phoenician glass industry.

The mountains of Lebanon stretch for 100 miles (160 kilometers) in the east.

Natural Plants, Animals, and Birds

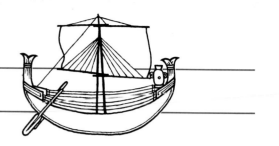

Dense forests of pine, cypress, oak, fir, and the famous conifer, the Cedar of Lebanon (*cedrus libani*) covered the Phoenician lands. Timber, used for furniture, major buildings, and ship-building, was widely traded.

Animal life was varied. Panthers, bears, hyenas, wolves, jackals, and hares lived in the mountains, as well as smaller animals, such as squirrels, dormice, and martens.

The sea provided plenty of fish, including the famous murex shellfish (called the *murex trunculus* or *murex brandaris*). The Phoenicians learned to extract a purple dye from this shell to color cloth, which they traded at high prices.

Birds in the mountains included eagles, buzzards, kites, falcons, and hawks. Phoenicia had other birds as well. They included owls, kingfishers, and migrating birds such as flamingoes, pelicans, cormorants, herons, and snipes.

Below and opposite: the eagle and wolf are some of the animals that inhabit the mountains of Lebanon.

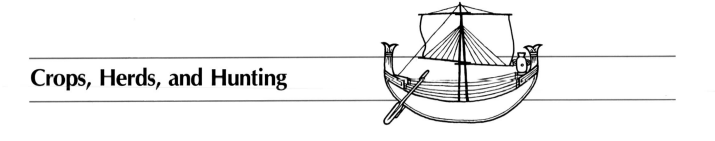

Crops, Herds, and Hunting

In the fertile valleys and lowlands, the Phoenicians grew wheat, olives, vines, and fruit trees, especially figs and **sycamores.** Palms grew abundantly. **Flax** was cultivated. The hillsides were terraced and irrigated. Phoenician engineers built dams and bridges, using huge blocks of stone. Remains of Phoenician dams can be seen at Aradus, Sidon, and Tyre. The Phoenicians had irrigation systems for bringing water to dry farmlands before 1500 B.C. It is thought that the Phoenicians taught their irrigation methods to other people of the Mediterranean whom they encountered on trading voyages.

The most common domesticated animals were donkeys, oxen, sheep, and goats. Carvings show that the Phoenicians tilled the lands with a simple plow drawn by oxen. Fish was a main source of protein in the people's diet. Domestic animals increased in variety as Phoenicians traded with other **nomadic** and **seminomadic** tribes. Many animals, including elephants, were raised in the Phoenician city of carthage in North Africa. In later years the Carthaginian army of Hannibal used elephants in battle.

Ruins of the Phoenician Harbor at Byblos.

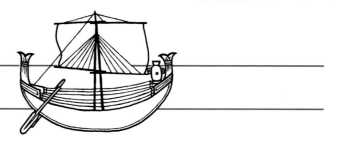

How Families Lived

The Phoenicians left few written records, especially about their personal lives. Their art, sculpture, coins, temple ruins, and inscriptions give us some idea of how some of the people lived. We know about trading activities and colonies from the writings of neighboring peoples and more distant trading nations. About their family life we can only guess.

Phoenician Men

Phoenician men worked at many different trades and occupations. Most Phoenicians were farmers, working the fertile land with a one-toothed plow and a draft animal. But the Phoenicians who lived along the rocky coast often became sailors and traders. Sailors in the merchant fleet would usually be away for long periods of time. This was also a dangerous job, since many ships sank during their trading trips.

Skilled craftsmen supported these traders by turning the land's wealth of natural resources into prized products. Some of the most sought-after products were colorful clothing; engraved, metal bowls; and furniture inlaid with ivory. The Phoenicians were also well known throughout the ancient world for their skill as builders.

As in any culture, men were also needed to work as religious leaders, government officials, and local merchants.

Phoenician houses.

Carthaginian coin, third century B.C. Coins give us an idea of how the Phoenicians lived and what they looked liked.

118152

Phoenician Women

Women are rarely mentioned in the literature or shown in art. There is no evidence to show that women had rights to go to sea in the trading ships but they certainly accompanied their husbands overseas to start up new colonies and trading communities. Occasionally, we get glimpses of women taking part in the life of the temples, but very little else.

We can assume that women did what all women did in antiquity; they cared for the children, managed the household, and prepared the food. They gathered wood and assisted their husbands in sowing seed and harvesting the crops. They milked the cows and goats, and tended the chickens. They churned butter and cooked the meals. They weaved cloth and made clothes. In early times, some made pottery vessels. Perhaps they plastered mud-brick houses, as women do in Syria today.

We are told that children were sacrificed to the gods, but we are not told what mothers thought of this custom or how they coped with the loss of a child. And we know nothing of how the children were educated, what games they played, or even the names they might have been called.

Houses

The Assyrians wrote about the Phoenician houses of two stories that had windows, **balustrades,** and palm-shaped columns. Also, houses in Carthage were reported to be six stories high. Based on their renowned craftsmanship, wealthy Phoenician homes were filled with luxury goods. The prophet Ezekiel mentions the Phoenician houses being "pleasant," meaning luxurious.

Because Phoenician towns were built over by other civilizations, very little remains. However, there is one town near Cape Bon that was not built over and archaeologists have found that these houses were well-built with thick walls, cement floors, and brick roofs. They had bathrooms and drains.

Opposite: Phoenician youth with lotus.

Below: Phoenicians extracted dye from the shellfish murex, which they used for making their famous purple cloth.

Food and Medicine

The Phoenicians grew wheat, olives, vines, fruit trees, and dates. Archaeologists have uncovered large stone wheels, which were used for grinding wheat grain into flour. Other large stones with holes have also been found. These stones were probably olive and grape presses, used to make olive oil and wine.

Vegetables such as cabbages, thistles, garlic, peas, and lentils were also grown. Fish was eaten as a main source of protein, and salt was obtained by evaporating sea water.

In the Phoenician cities and on the islands, rainwater was collected for drinking and kept in large cisterns. The people who lived at Aradus used a freshwater spring that gushed into the sea. They inserted a lead funnel into the spring, and, on the end of the funnel, they attached a leather tube. This tube carried the freshwater supply for the island's inhabitants.

Remains of clay and wooden bowls have been found, along with clay water pitchers. Food was mostly eaten by hand, but spoons, which were used either for serving or eating, have been found.

Medicine

Information about the medical knowledge of the Phoenicians is scant, but Phoenician medicine was no doubt similar to that of other countries whose literary texts dealt with medicine. Natural substances: garlic, olive oil, weeds of various kinds, frankincense, and myrrh were taken internally and applied externally in salves and poultices. Based on archaeological evidence in Israel from the late fifth century

Phoenician jug from 1200 B.C., probably used as a water pitcher.

B.C. surgery was performed on the skull, probably to relieve pressure in the brain. Special tools for removing foreign material from the eye was part of every family's medicine chest.

Clothes

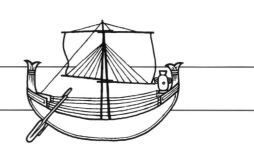

The main industry of the Phoenicians was textiles. Wool and linen were woven into cloth. The Phoenicians were famous for their use of purple dye. The name *Phoenicia* is thought to come from a Greek word meaning purple dye. The colors extracted from the murex shellfish ranged from pink to dark violet. In ancient times, such colored fabric was rare. It was regarded as a luxury item and could be sold at a high price. The cloth dyed the deepest shade of violet was so valuable that it was called "royal purple" and was only worn by kings and other rulers.

Men

Sculptures have been found that show men wearing belted pleated skirts ornamented on the front with two large **uraei** clasps. Large necklaces or pendants of a sovereign or god were worn by men. Other sculptures show men in loin clothes (short skirts) and tight-fitting tunics reaching to the ankles. Men are shown on tiles and frescoes wearing multi-colored clothes with embroidered borders. Conical-shaped caps seem to have been worn by most men, who also seem to have preferred long hair and beards.

Women

Again, sculpture is the best indicator of what Phoenician women wore. The main garment seems to have been a long tunic tied with a belt with two tassels. However, another sculpture shows a woman in a flounced skirt. Some sculptures show a low circular headdress and tight necklaces. Hair was also plaited down the back with two short side plaits.

In Phoenician Malta, fine women's clothes,

Sculptures found by archaeologists give us some idea of how the Phoenicians dressed. This bust of a Phoenician woman shows her in a headdress, wearing many necklaces, and with a cape draped over her shoulders.

soft hats, and cushions are mentioned in the records.

Capes were worn by both men and women.

Gold and silver jewelry has been found in Phoenician tombs. Pendants, earrings, bracelets, **diadems,** and smaller objects in gold and ivory, including pins, hair pins, and combs, were found.

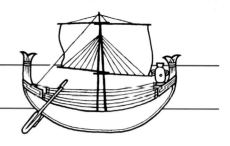

Religion and Rituals of the Phoenicians

Historians and archaeologists have had difficulty finding out about Phoenician religion. Only a few writings have been found, and most of these are only fragments. Inscriptions, coins, scattered writings, and later writings of the Greeks and Romans have helped. A Christian historian, Eusebius, in the fourth century A.D. studied the work of Philo of Byblos. Eusebius found that it included the work of a Phoenician priest, called Sanchuniathon, whose writing has given some more information. The **Ugaritic Texts,** written in an alphabetic script using **cuneiform** wedges on clay tablets were found in 1929 and include religious texts, myths, **incantations,** rituals, and lists of offerings and gods. These texts have extended our knowledge of Phoenician religion. The texts are from Ugarit, the ancient name of the city where the tablets were found. The language is North Canaanite, which is closely related to later Phoenician and Hebrew.

Temples

Open-air and closed temples were built. Temples were considered to be places where the gods dwelled. Each temple had a porch, a chapel, and a **betyl,** and the altar was the most holy place. There was usually a sacred fountain or bowl. Shrines were located in the elaborate temples. Around places of worship were statues of gods, as well as small figurines thought to be fertility goddesses, and figures of winged lions with human heads (**sphinxes**) that served as guardians. Religion and beliefs varied slightly from city to city.

At Ugarit the king and queen were important religious figures and offerings were made to them. A chief priest and other priests carried out religious ceremonies. Temple singers, priestesses, and other helpers such as

Above: ivory box lid from Ras-Shamrah, Ugarit.

Opposite: ruins of the Phoenician temple of Obelisks at Byblos, 1900 B.C.

"drawers of water" were present in the temples. The temple also controlled the land, so priests had administrative, as well as religious duties.

Nature

Natural elements, water, groves of trees, and rocks were considered sacred, and rituals were performed near them. Fire played an important part in religious ceremonies, and a sacred flame was kept burning in some temples.

Some Phoenician Gods and Goddesses

Name	About the God	Name	About the God
El	El is the head of the gods and his wife is Ashirat. He is father of all the gods except Baal, and also the creator of man. Phoenician texts also say "Creator of the Earth," which is expanded in the Bible to "maker of heaven and earth." There are varying impressions and descriptions of El, one of which is an old man with a long gray beard. Sometimes he is shown with four wings and two faces.	Ashirat or Asherah	"She who walks on the Sea" and also called "Holiness." (The name, Asherah, frequently appears in the Bible but refers to a wooden object used in the worship of this goddess.)
Dagon or Dagan	This is the next most important god on the list but the meaning of the name is uncertain. Dagon is associated with fertility of crops, particularly wheat and corn. Dagon later became the chief god of the Philistines.	Astarte	A goddess of love, fertility, and war. Referred to as Ashtoreth in the Bible.
Baal or Hadad	The storm god, the "cloud rider." He is the son of Dagon and is sometimes called "the Prince" and "the Conquering One." He is often shown riding on a bull or brandishing a mace or thunderbolts. He was also the patron god of Carthage.	Anath	The chief Ugaritic goddess of love, fertility, and war who was very fierce in battle and is often shown wading in blood and wearing heads and hands as ornaments.
		Mot	God of the dead, the son of El and Ashirat.
Baalat	Whose name means "lady" was associated with the city of Byblos. There are inscriptions begging Baalat to prolong the years of the kings of Byblos. She is thought of as the earth mother and as a goddess of fertility.	Melquart or Melkarth	Patron god of Tyre and later the head of the Pantheon at Carthage. His name means "the king of the (underworld) city." His name has been found on many inscriptions but scholars do not yet know very much about him.
Yarikh	A male moon god.	Adonis (also called Eshmun)	His name means "lord." He was a young god of vegetation, doomed to spend half the year in the underworld and the other half on earth, symbolizing seasonal cycles. One myth tells of how his beauty caught the attention of the love goddess, Aphrodite, whose lover, Ares, became jealous. One day while Adonis was hunting, Ares took the form of a wild boar and attacked Adonis, who then bled to death. His blood stained the River Adonis (though minerals in the water made it red). Women took part in regular mournings for him, and special Adonis Gardens were set out in his honor.
Kothar or Khasis	A Canaanite craftsman god whose name means "skillful" or "clever."		

Customs and Ceremonies

The Phoenicians made sacrifices to their gods, using animals, birds, and people. The **topheth** was the name given to the place where human sacrifices were made. Funeral urns have been found in many places and the topheth at Carthage was used throughout the history of that city. One writer describes a human sacrifice in which the victim was placed in the hands of a bronze statue and dropped into flames. Children were frequently sacrificed, and although this seems to have been regarded as a very important part of the Phoenician religion, archaeologists still are not sure why. It is known that sacrifices at Ugarit were made at the time of the new moon and on the fourteenth day of the month.

Feasts

The Phoenicians celebrated feasts to mark religious and agricultural events. Feasts at Ugarit included unleavened bread, weeks (Pentacost), and booths, which are thought to have been harvest feasts originally. Other festivals honored the gods, particularly Adonis, and writers, such as Theocritus, referred to

Phoenician fertility goddess made from ivory.

Model of a Phoenician temple, built during the Greek period.

such festivals as reenactments of the funerals of the gods.

Burial

The Phoenicians believed in an afterlife. Funeral offerings were buried with the dead, whose bodies were also **embalmed.** Sometimes the body was placed in a large limestone or marble sarcophagus, elaborately decorated on all sides, and closed with a gabled stone roof. Tombs have been excavated at many places, including Sidon, Amrit, and Carthage. Tombs were built underground with corridors called **dromos** leading to them. Monuments called **meghazils** were built above ground over the tombs.

Obeying the Law

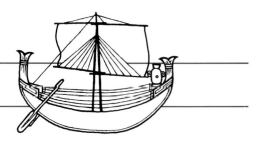

The lawmakers in a society are the people who govern the society. Each Phoenician city was independent and was governed by its own king. Kings were assisted by a council of ancients who often made decisions if the king was absent. It is thought that these ancients were the leading merchants or members of the city's leading families who controlled the trade. A governor supervised the administration and court of the city.

Priests had administrative duties as well as religious duties. In some places the estates of land were controlled from the temple. Some priests also had duties such as "chief priest of shepherds," which meant they looked after the temple flocks.

At Carthage

Phoenician colonies, or city-states, did not always retain the same kind of government as the Phoenician homeland's. About half-way through the sixth century B.C., the governing of Carthage seems to have been divided between a king and a senate. The king's duty was to summon the senate and preside over it.

Aristotle, writing in the fourth century B.C., wrote of a government of two magistrates, a senate of 300 and a court of 104. This system continued until the Romans took control of Carthage in 149 B.C.

The Phoenicians, in spite of having used an alphabet, have left no written code of their laws; therefore, we do not know what activities were regarded as crimes, or what penalties were imposed as punishments.

What we do know of Phoenician law comes from texts that occasionally mention Phoenician law. One law, of which little is known, is now referred to as Rhodian Law. This law dates back to the Phoenicians and was named after the island of Rhodes in the Mediterranean. This law referred to the loss of cargo and ships. If a cargo had to be thrown overboard to stop a ship from sinking, the losses would be shared both by owners of the ship and owners of the cargo under terms that were mutually agreeable. Today, this law is known in maritime law as gross average.

Detail from King Hiram's tomb. King Hiram of Tyre was the Phoenician king who built Solomon's Temple for King Solomon in Jerusalem.

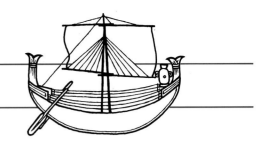

Writing It Down: Recording Things

Alphabet

The Canaanites at Ugarit in the fifteenth century B.C. used Mesopotamian cuneiform writing. The Phoenicians, however, wrote in a **semitic** alphabetic script that resembled early Hebrew script. This alphabet was taught to people with whom the Phoenicians traded, including the Greeks. The Greeks in turn adopted the alphabet and adapted it for their own purposes. Among the Phoenicians, the alphabet's main use was for recording business transactions.

Phoenician inscriptions have been found at many sites. One example is a bronze cup from Cyprus, called the Baal of Lebanon (now in the Louvre, Paris), which dates from about 800 B.C. The earliest Phoenician inscription to be deciphered dates from the eleventh century B.C.

Language

The Phoenician language was very similar to Hebrew and Moabite. Gradually, the language spread as Phoenician colonies were established. A later form of Phoenician, known as Neo-Punic (*Punic* means "Phoenician"), was still spoken fairly widely in the fourth century B.C. in places such as the hills near Hippo Regius.

Writing Materials

With the development of the alphabet, **papyrus** replaced clay as a writing material and **seals** came into common use. Often these seals were fitted into rings and worn by the owner to identify himself, just as we use signatures to identify ourselves. Common designs included winged sphinxes, lions squatting on podiums, goats, falcons, gods with animal heads, figures of a man with a stick, and crescent moons.

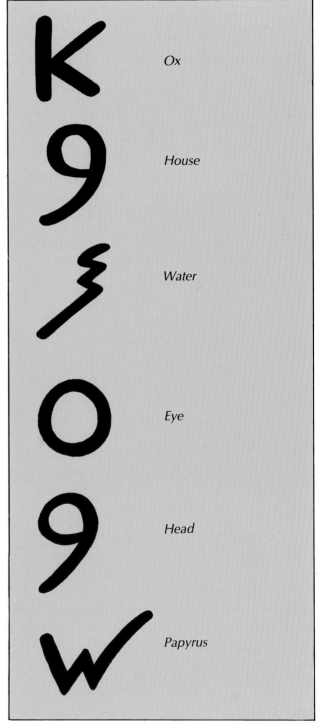

K	Ox
9	House
ﾐ	Water
O	Eye
9	Head
W	Papyrus

Phoenician writing symbols c. 1000 B.C.

Weights and Measures

It is thought that the Phoenicians (as well as the Hittities, Assyrians, and Israelites) derived their system of measurement from the Babylonians and Egyptians, but what these measures were is not known.

Above: tablet from 2100 B.C. showing cuneiform, Mesopotamian writing used by the Phoenicians, and also the Sumerians.

Opposite: Most of our information about the Phoenicians comes from the contact they made with neighboring countries in the course of trade.

Phoenician Legends

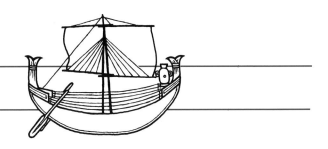

Though the Phoenicians developed an alphabet and taught it to others, they did not write about themselves. The Phoenicians were merchants and traders, concerned with money and material things. They were not interested in literary pursuits. Every culture has its legends and folklore, which are passed on by word-of-mouth from one generation to another. If the Phoenicians had a folklore and legends, sadly, because these legends were not written down, we now know nothing of them.

Writers like Homer, Herodotus, Xenophon, and Flaubert, from other cultures and ages, have given us glimpses into the lives of the Phoenicians.

From Homer's *Odyssey* we learn about conditions of seafaring in the days when the Phoenicians were becoming powerful.

Herodotus, who wrote after Homer, tried to reconstruct, in words, the world of the Phoenicians. He describes, for example, activities of the Phoenician traders as they made their way along the Mediterranean ports.

After Herodotus, the Greek writer Xenophon described a visit he made to a Phoenician merchant ship. He described the ship as neat, efficient, and in perfect order.

French writer Gustave Flaubert, after studying history and archaeology, tried to depict accurately life in Carthage, in his novel *Salammbo*.

We must be content with the accounts of writers, for the Phoenicians, themselves, left us no folk heroes, heroines, or stories of adventure.

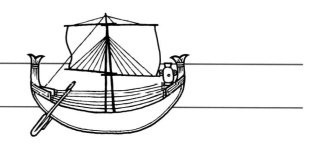

Art and Architecture

Information about Phoenician art and architecture comes to us in indirect ways. Archaeological finds in Phoenician lands have been few. Most Phoenician art has been found in other lands.

Phoenician gold ax, which shows the same design found on bronzed axes used in warfare.

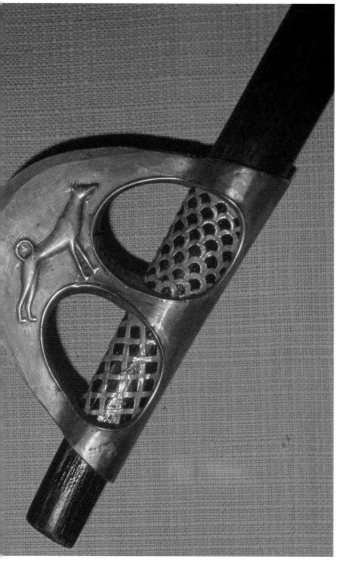

Temples

No parts of temples remain in what used to be Phoenicia, but we do have knowledge of temples built by the Phoenicians in other lands. The Temple of King Solomon, in Jerusalem, was built by the Phoenicians, using Phoenician designs, in the tenth century B.C. Unfortunately, the temple was destroyed when the Babylonians conquered Jerusalem in 597 B.C. The writings of the historian Herodotus describe some Phoenician temples, and the pictures of some temples appear on coins.

Remains of Phoenician shrines have been found at Tell Sugas, Sidon, Amrit, and Ain El Hayat, some of which have inscriptions and sacred ceremonial bowls.

Towns

Assyrian writing has revealed Phoenician cities to us, describing them as surrounded by walls with **turrets** and **battlements.** Reliefs of Sennacherib depict a Phoenician town with walls and two-story houses. The top story has windows with balustrades and miniature palm-shaped columns. Similar houses have been carved on ivory by the Phoenicians.

Opposite: Phoenician glass bottle. Glassware was a typical Phoenician craft in which a high level of skill was achieved. Phoenician glassware demanded a high price in trade.

Decorated Metal Bowls

Metal bowls date from the eighth and seventh centuries B.C., and Egyptian, as well as Mesopotamian and Aegean influences, are apparent in the kind of decoration.

Glassware

Glassmaking was known to the Egyptians and others, but a much higher level of skill was attained by the Phoenicians. They were able to produce transparent glass that was much better than the opaque glass of the Egyptians. By the first century B.C., glassblowing was developed and hollow glass vessels and ornaments were produced.

Wood Carving

Not many examples of fine Phoenician wood carving remain, as these have perished over time. Phoenician craftsmen excelled in wood carving, and many of the molds used to make bronze statues were of wood.

Masks

Terracotta masks have been found in the Phoenician city of Carthage and consist of smiling female faces and grimacing male faces. While some of these masks are life-size and could have been worn in ancient dramas, many are quite small, and could not have been worn over the face. It is thought that they were buried in tombs with the dead. Other masks, grotesque in feature, are thought to represent demons.

Opposite: a model of Solomon's Temple. Phoenician skill and labor were used to build Solomon's Temple in Jerusalem for the Hebrews.
Right: seated bronze figure of a goddess (thought to be Astarte) draped with snakes.

Sculpture

Small bronze sculptures and stone sculptures have been found of figures thought to be kings or gods. These sculptures are in many ways similar to the Egyptian statues. Many of these sculptures show a figure in the company of lions, or holding papyrus reeds or **lotus** flowers, which are characteristics of Egyptian are. Some headdresses resemble the crowns of Egyptians. Many winged sphinxes have been found. Some of them wear the Egyptian double crown.

Between the fourth and the fifth centuries B.C., a definite Greek influence appears in Phoenician sculpture.

Going Places: Transportation, Exploration, and Communication

Because the Phoenician coast was narrow, hemmed in by hills, and not suitable for farming, the Phoenicians turned to the sea and became seafarers of the ancient world. Their ships were of two types, warships and traders. The warships were about 82 feet (25 meters) long with a **convex** stern, and were fitted with underwater rams, used to damage and sink enemy vessels. Warships had two and three banks of oars under a deck in which the Phoenician warriors' shields were hung. Warships were fitted with a high mast to support triangular sails.

Below: Phoenician traders. Their wares included purple cloth, glassware, and jewelry. Phoenician traders traveled great distances by sea.

Opposite: Phoenician trade map.

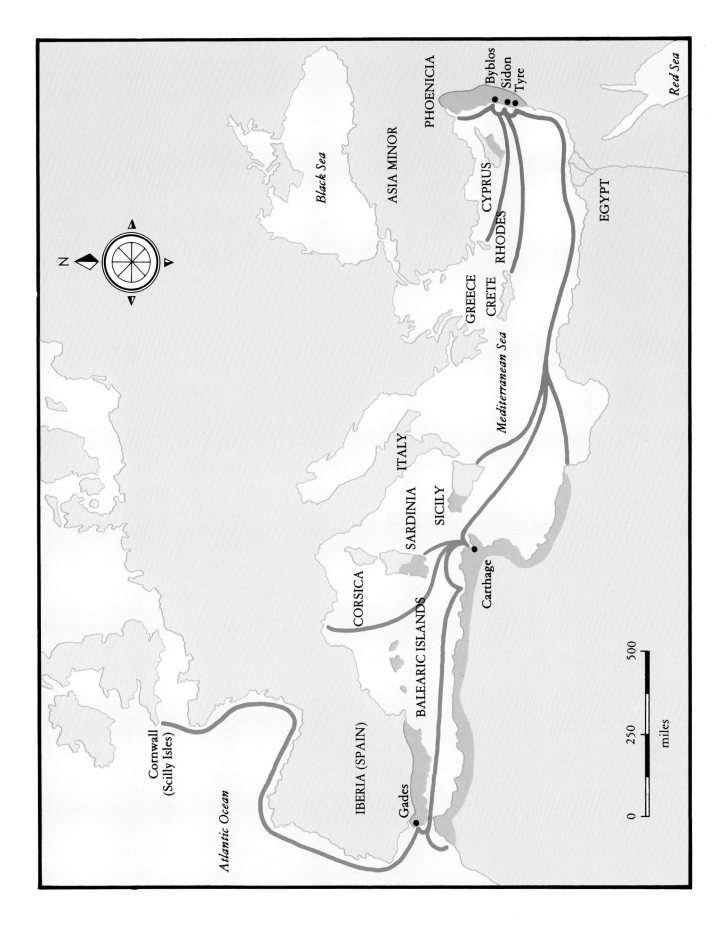

Red Sea

Byblos
Sidon
Tyre
PHOENICIA

Black Sea

ASIA MINOR

CYPRUS

RHODES

EGYPT

GREECE
CRETE

Mediterranean Sea

N

ITALY

SARDINIA

SICILY

CORSICA

Carthage

BALEARIC ISLANDS

Atlantic Ocean

Cornwall
(Scilly Isles)

IBERIA (SPAIN)

Gades

0   250   500

miles

Initially, trading ships (which were sometimes defended by warships) were built with a convex prow and stern and had two banks of oars and no mast. Later, a new type of trading ship was devised, which had a round hull and a heavy keel and a post at stem and stern. A single square sail was used for power. The large crew of rowers was eliminated, as people took up valuable cargo space and also had to be fed.

Minor trading ships were much smaller, with a single bank of oars but with no room for soldiers. These ships were possibly used for less valuable cargo.

Although the Phoenicians traveled great distances by sea, most of their routes were within sight of land, and they made use of sheltered coves and anchorages at night. On some longer voyages, the Phoenicians were known to kidnap people to sell into the slave markets.

Although the total number of Phoenician colonies is not known, it is thought to have been at least fifty. Some of these colonies developed into great cities, such as Carthage, which became a powerful trading center in its own right. Other important centers included Byblos, Beirut, Sidon, and Tyre. The Phoenicians were essentially traders, not empire builders. They did not intend to set up colonies, so large numbers of people could emigrate from the homeland. They needed new markets, ports, and raw materials, in particular, copper from Cyprus, silver, iron, and tin from Spain. The Phoenicians had strong trading ties with Egypt, which explains the Egyptian influences in other aspects of Phoenician life, particularly art.

Relief of Phoenician trading ship. This ship is of the type used in later times that was powered by a single square mast.

Famous Phoenician Voyages

According to Herodotus, the Greek historian, Pharoah Necko of Egypt (609–593 B.C.) persuaded the Phoenicians to circumnavigate (sail around) Africa, requiring just less than three years.

In 530 B.C. a Phoenician general named Hanno sailed from Carthage and set a course for the south. Besides the crew, on board were men and women who were to establish agricultural and commercial colonies along the Atlantic coast of Africa. They finally reached what is now Cape Juba, and continued along the coast, coming close to the equator near the Cameroons. Hanno wrote about his voyage even further south, where he met, "savages…with coarse hairy skins" never seen before. He was probably seeing chimpanzees for the first time.

Admiral Himilco also set out from Carthage to identify tin mines in what is now Cornwall in England. It is thought that he reached Cornwall and made trade agreements with the people.

Phoenicia's Neighbors

The Phoenicians developed good relations with the neighboring Israelites. King Hiram of Tyre sent King David craftsmen and supplied cedar to build his palace. King Solomon (David's successor) was also provided with materials and craftsmen to build his temple, a palace, and a fleet. In return, Hiram received gifts of grain, wine, oil, and twenty towns in Galilee.

In later times Ittoball of Tyre consented to the marriage of his daughter Jezebel to Ahab, son of Omri of Israel, and both cultures influenced each other. Later, though, the Hebrew prophets bitterly denounced the Phoenicians of Tyre. With the prophet Elijah as the leader, a bloody revolution took place that wiped out Ahab, Jezebel, and their family.

Music, Dancing, and Recreation

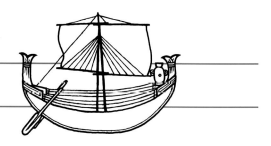

Though we know little about Phoenician music and dancing, we can presume they were part of the culture. All cultures have some form of music and dancing, which is usually a necessary part of religious rituals and festivals. In Phoenicia, there were probably temple dancers and musicians who played instruments, such as pipes, cymbals, and drums.

All Near Eastern weddings both today and in antiquity featured communal dancing. Even funerals had professional women who wailed and danced.

Musical instruments can be found on various pieces of Phoenician sculpture originating from the island of Sardinia. On one **stele** (an inscribed slab or pillar), from the island town of Nora, is a picture of a goddess dressed in a long robe and holding a tambourine. Tambourines are also shown in the hands of figures on **icons** in Sulcis, another island town. Statues showing women holding lyres have also been found. One Phoenician inscription found in an Egyptian temple reads: "I am Psr, son of Baalyanton, the kettledrum player."

Stele showing Phoenicians with musical instruments, which included the tambourine, the lyre, and pipes.

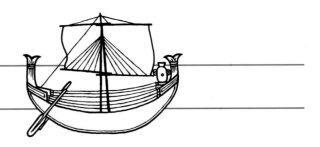

Wars and Battles

The Phoenicians built their cities for defense. They often chose sites on offshore islands or on the coast where there were natural bays or rivers for trading fleets and warships. To protect such settlements, they commonly surrounded the town with a large fortified wall. Phoenician cities in the west, however, raised large armies to protect their farflung colonies against the Greeks and Romans.

While the expansion of the western Phoenicians brought them into conflict with the Greeks, the Phoenicians of the east continued as traders, although the Phoenician homeland had become part of the great Persian Empire.

Detail showing part of a Phoenician warship. Scene from Semacherib's expedition to Phoenicia and Palestine in 702 B.C.

Alexander the Great and the Siege of Tyre 332 B.C.

When Alexander the Great made his great eastward sweep of conquests, he needed to cross the Phoenician lands after the Persians had conquered them. The city of Tyre, built on an island, resisted the attacks of Alexander's army for seven months. Eventually Alexander's army built a solid bridge from the mainland to the island and brought heavy artillery across the bridge to siege and conquer the city. Alexander's capture of Tyre destroyed the power of the Phoenicians in the east.

First Punic War 264–241 B.C.

In 264 B.C. Carthage established a garrison at Messina on the island of Sicily to protect her trade route from pirates and to complete a chain of island trading posts along the Mediterranean. The Romans saw this strong fighting force close to Italy as a threat and sent troops into Sicily, but these troops were only partially successful in destroying the Carthaginian forces. In 260 B.C. the Romans built their first fleet of battleships. A second fleet reached Africa after defeating the Carthaginian fleet. Eventually the Carthaginians ceded Sicily and the Lipari Islands to the Romans.

Second Punic War 218–201 B.C.

Hamilcar, the Carthaginian general, created a new settlement in Spain and the Romans again declared war on the Carthaginians in 218 B.C. The Carthaginian army was led by the Phoenician general Hannibal across the Pyrenees into southern Gaul, across the Alps and into Italy. With this army he soundly defeated the Romans, in 217 B.C., at the Battle of Lake Trasimene. He won another battle against the Romans the following year. Gradually the Carthaginian army began to weaken. Hannibal was ordered to return to Carthage. Eventually Carthage was attacked and conquered by the Romans. At the end of the Third Punic War, 149–146 B.C., the city was razed (burned) to the ground and the inhabitants of Carthage were sold into slavery.

Alexander the Great from Greece captured the Phoenician city of Tyre in 332 B.C.

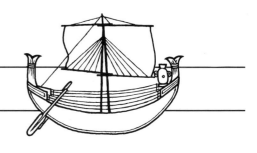

Phoenician Inventions and Special Skills

Alphabet

One of the greatest achievements of the Phoenicians was to teach their alphabet to people of the Mediterranean. The Greeks adopted this alphabet but reversed the facing of some letters because Phoenicians wrote from left to right. The Greeks also adapted some of the Semitic consonants to their own Indo-European sounds. But, the basic model remains the same and, in turn, is the model passed to the Romans and to the rest of Europe. Today this alphabet is used throughout Europe, America, and many other areas of the world.

Spread of Culture and Commodities

The Phoenicians provided the first channel of communication of culture from east to west. As well as teaching the alphabet to others, the Phoenicians taught other things, such as religious ideas. They also bought goods from people in the east, goods that were unknown but useful to people in the west and vice versa. Knowledge of other places, people, and inventions was also exchanged by the Phoenicians.

City-states

The city-state was a typical Phoenician political system whereby each city or colony was made self-governing. The Phoenicians did not attempt to govern all their colonies from a homeland city as other people had tried to do. Independent city-states were a more efficient form of government, as people could take care of their own local and immediate problems. The Greeks later used the same system to run their political affairs.

Colonization

The Phoenicians were the first people to establish colonies throughout the Mediterranean world. Previously, Phoenicians had remained in their homeland and used whatever resources could be found for trading with neighbors. As the country grew, the Phoenicians established their own colonies and ports. These ports not only provided safe anchorage for ships, but ensured a regular supply of raw materials needed for making goods and supplying markets.

Phoenician colonies were independent of the homeland and were self-governing. Some colonies were ruled by kings and others by wealthy merchants. The Phoenicians established their colonies along the north African coast and the Atlantic coast of North Africa in Spain and on the islands of Corsica, Sicily, Sardinia, and Cyprus.

Trading Skills

The Phoenicians' concept of trade was different from that of other people in the ancient world. Phoenicians created goods especially for trade. They bought goods for a low price in one place so that they could be sold in other places for a higher price. Phoenicians also understood that people would pay a higher price for goods that were scarce. They kept the monopoly on the supply of purple cloth, for example, by keeping the source of the purple dye a secret. They also kept the locations of their tin sources a secret, and the Romans tried various techniques to learn their secrets. Phoenicians were very skilled at understanding what people would be likely to buy.

Building Safe Cities

The Phoenicians sometimes built their cities in places that were safe from easy capture so that few armed soldiers were needed to repel an attack. Tyre resisted the efficient and large army of Alexander the Great for seven months.

Export of Crafts

Jewlery, ivory, metal, and glass were items of trade and not just items produced for use by people of the homeland. Production was intended for trade. Glasswork was a highly regarded Phoenician craft that enabled Phoenicians to produce transparent iridescent glass bowls, bottles, and flasks. These were unique products that commanded a high price.

Shipbuilding

The Phoenicians would not have been great traders and colonizers if they had not been able to build superior ships to carry them safely. The trading ships had a round hull to increase cargo space for the products to be traded. The warships, on the other hand, were long and narrow, for increased speed and maneuverability. Carvings, sculptures, and coins survive to show us what these ships were like.

Below: the Phoenicians designed superior ships for trade and warfare. Warships like the one shown below were propelled by oars.

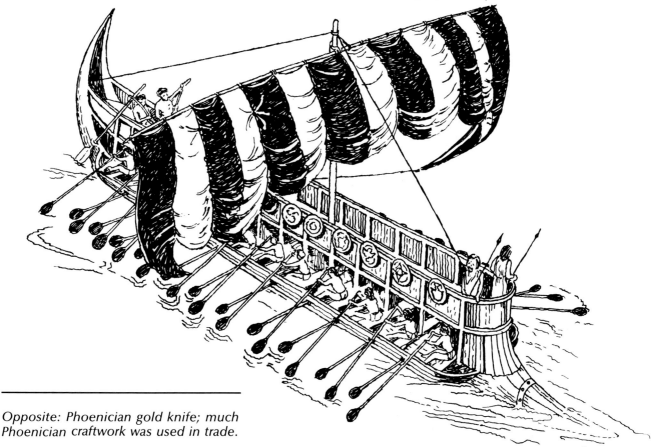

Opposite: Phoenician gold knife; much Phoenician craftwork was used in trade.

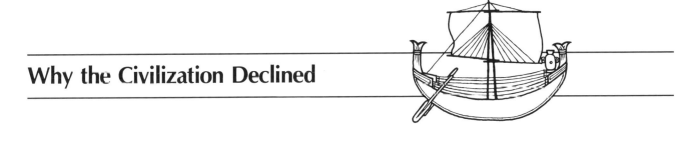

Why the Civilization Declined

The Phoenician lands were gradually taken over by military conquest. The conquering people absorbed and overshadowed the Phoenician civilization and culture. The Phoenician cities were not united as an empire. Various people attacked these independent cities and one by one, they were taken over by people with larger and more powerful armies.

The Phoenician cities that were established in the west, along the north African coast, continued as prosperous and thriving centers but eventually suffered defeats. First the Greeks took Sicily and dominated the area. After the Greeks, the Romans conquered and made these lands part of their empire. In the east the Persians conquered and occupied the Phoenician cities. Following this, Alexander the Great captured the eastern city of Tyre. The Egyptian city of Alexandria replaced Tyre as the leading trade center of the Mediterranean.

The great Phoenician civilization was gradually conquered and its culture dominated by that of its conquerors. However, most of these conquerors understood how advanced this civilization was and learned a great deal from it. They adopted and adapted many aspects of Phoenician culture, so it did not completely die out.

Lebanon today.

Glossary

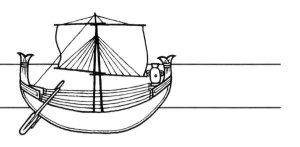

Balustrade A railing above a series of short pillars on a building or a porch.

Battlements Parapets or small enclosures with a series of openings originally for shooting through. Battlements were placed around cities and houses so they could be defended if armies attacked.

Betyl A sacred stone usually standing and sometimes trimmed into a conical shape.

Canaanite One of the names used by ancient Phoenicians; also, Hebrew for *merchant.*

Convex Curved like a circle or sphere when viewed from the outside; bulging and curved.

Cuneiform Writing having wedge-shaped characters and used in ancient Persia, Assyria, Babylonia, Egypt, and Phoenicia before the introduction of the Phoenician alphabet. The wedges were made with a triangular stylus pressed into wet clay.

Diadem A crown or a headband adorned with jewels. It was often worn by those in authority, kings, and other dignitaries.

Dromos Corridors of underground tombs.

Embalmed Treated with spices, oils, and other preservatives in an attempt to prevent natural decay.

Flax An annual plant with blue flowers. The fiber of this plant is made into linen yarn and woven fabrics.

Incantation A chant or special words spoken or sung in religious ceremonies, which were believed to have special powers.

Icon Picture, image, or other representation on sculpture or stele.

Lignite A type of coal with a dark brown color and woody texture.

Lotus A plant similar to a water lily.

Meghazils Above-ground monuments of underground tombs.

Nomadic Not having a permanent place of living; wandering from place to place usually in search of animals and plants for food.

Papyrus A form of paper made from the fiber of the stem of the papyrus reed, which grew in the Nile Valley. Writing on papyrus was done with a reed pen dipped in ink.

Promontory A high point of land or rock projecting into the sea. A headland is a promontory.

Seal A special or official sign of someone in authority, such as a king, placed on a document. The design of the seal was easily identified and the seal itself often set into a ring and worn by the person for safekeeping. Soft wax or mud was placed on the document or vessel and the design of the seal imprinted to leave a mark.

Semi-nomadic Having a semi-permanent place of living for a part of the year but having to move to other places in search of food before being able to return.

Semitic A family of ancient Near Eastern languages including Aramaic, Hebrew, Phoenician, and Ugaritic.

Sphinx An imaginary creature usually with the head of a person and the body of a lion. The Phoenicians frequently depicted a winged sphinx on bowls.

Stele A standing block of stone bearing an inscription or sculptural design.

Sycamore A fruit-bearing tree similar to a fig.

Topheth A place where human sacrifices were made to the gods by the Phoenicians.

Turrets Small towers on a larger building.

Ugaritic Texts Alphabetic texts written on clay tablets with a wedge-shaped stylus, found at Ugarit (Ras Shamra) on the Syrian coast in 1929.

Uraei Sacred asp or cobra clasps.

The Phoenicians: Some Famous People and Places

TYRE

Tyre, an ancient Phoenician city, still exists today and is situated on the coast of modern Lebanon. Tyre was built on an island and was a major Phoenician seaport and trade center. In the ninth century B.C. colonists from Tyre founded the city of Carthage in north Africa. During the seventh–eighth centuries B.C. Tyre was subject to Assyrian domination, and in 585–573 B.C. the Babylonians, under Nebuchadnezzar, besieged it. However, the most famous siege of Tyre was that carried out by Alexander the Great, in 322 B.C. After seven months of attempting to take the city without success, Alexander built a floating causeway from Tyre to the mainland, over which his troops marched to finally attack and capture the city. 10,000 people were put to death and 30,000 were sold into slavery after this battle.

SIDON

Sidon was an ancient Phoenician city founded in the third millennium B.C. Sidon was famous for its purple dye and glassware. Along with Aradus, Byblos, Tyre and Akka, Sidon was one of the great cities of the Phoenicians and it is thought that Sidon was the leading city until the tenth century. Homer and the Bible both use the word Sidonians to mean Phoenicians.

Stone coffins belonging to Eshmunazar and Tennes, two kings of Sidon during the Phoenician period, have been found. Details about Eshmunazar are vague but it is thought that he became king after his father's death, when he was still a child. The government was exercised by his mother initially. It is thought that Eshmunazar ruled some time during the fifth century.

Tennes was king of Sidon from 354 to 344 B.C., and led a revolt in 346 B.C. in which the palace and a royal park were sacked. The Persian Artaxerxes intervened and quelled the revolt, but Sidon was burned to the ground and over 40,000 people were killed. Tennes was also killed.

CARTHAGE

Carthage, founded by the Phoenicians of Tyre in 814 B.C. on the north coast of Africa, was built on a triangular peninsula with the Lake of Tunis providing safe anchorage. The peninsula was joined to the mainland by a narrow neck of land, thereby making it easy to defend. The ancient citadel, the Byrsa, was located in Carthage. Tombs have been found, together with cremated remains of children, sacrificed to the Carthaginian fertility goddess Tanit.

Carthage gained much of its wealth from agriculture and trade. The city came into conflict with Rome from 300 to 200 B.C., and fell to the Romans in 146 B.C. The city was then plundered and razed to the ground, but was later rebuilt by the Romans.